Spring Ha
Bible Workbook

DANIEL

Faith Under Fire

Elizabeth McQuoid

Series editor for Bible character workbooks – Ian Coffey

Authentic

SPRING HARVEST

Equipping the Church for action

First published in 2005 by Spring Harvest Publishing Division and Authentic Media
9 Holdom Avenue, Bletchley, Milton Keynes, Bucks, MK1 1QR, UK
and 129 Mobilization Drive, Waynesboro, GA 30830-4575, USA

www.authenticmedia.co.uk

British Library Cataloguing in Publication Data

A catalogue record for this book is available from the British Library

ISBN 1-85078-617-8

Typeset by Spring Harvest
Cover design by Diane Bainbridge
Print management by Adare Carwin
Printed and Bound by J. H. Haynes & Co. Ltd., Sparkford

CONTENTS

About this book   **4**

Introduction to Daniel   **7**

Session One: **Cooperation without compromise** Daniel 1   **8**

Session Two: **Ultimate triumph** Daniel 2   **13**

Session Three: **Faith under fire** Daniel 3   **20**

Session Four: **Heaven rules** Daniel 4   **26**

Session Five: **A play for power** Daniel 5   **32**

Session Six: **Tried and tested** Daniel 6   **38**

Leaders' Guide

Introduction   **44**

Session One   **47**

Session Two   **49**

Session Three   **51**

Session Four   **53**

Session Five   **55**

Session Six   **57**

Further information   **59**

ABOUT THIS BOOK

This workbook is written primarily for use in a group situation, but can easily be used by individuals who want to study the life of Daniel. It can be used in a variety of contexts, so it is perhaps helpful to spell out the assumptions that we have made about the groups that will use it. These can have a variety of names – home groups, Bible study groups, cell groups – we've used house group as the generic term.

- The emphasis of the studies will be on the application of the Bible. Group members will not just learn facts, but will be encouraged to think: 'How does this apply to me? What change does it require of me? What incidents or situations in my life is this relevant to?'
- House groups can encourage honesty and make space for questions and doubts. The aim of the studies is not to find the 'right answer', but to help members understand the Bible by working through the questions. The Christian faith throws up paradoxes. Events in people's lives may make particular verses difficult to understand. The house group should be a safe place to express these concerns.
- House groups can give opportunities for deep friendships to develop. Group members will be encouraged to talk about their experiences, feelings, questions, hopes and fears. They will be able to offer one another pastoral support and to get involved in each others' lives.
- There is a difference between being a collection of individuals who happen to meet together every Wednesday and being an effective group who bounce ideas off each other, spark inspiration and creativity and pool their talents and resources to create solutions together and whose whole is definitely greater than the sum of its parts. The process of working through these studies will encourage healthy group dynamics.

Space is given for you to write answers, comments, questions and thoughts. This book will not tell you what to think, but it will help you discover the truth of God's word through thinking, discussing, praying and listening.

The New International Version of the text is printed in the workbook. If you usually use a different version, then read from your own Bible as well.

Our Bible studies will look at the first six chapters of the book of Daniel. If you have time, you may like to read through these chapters, perhaps in a modern version such as *The Message*.

FOR GROUP MEMBERS

▶ You will get more out of the study if you spend some time during the week reading the passage and thinking about the questions. Make a note of anything you don't understand.

▶ Pray that God will help you to understand the passage and show you how to apply it. Pray for other members in the group too, that they will find the study helpful.

▶ Be willing to take part in the discussions. The leader of the group is not there as an expert with all the answers. They will want everyone to get involved and share their thoughts and opinions.

▶ However, don't dominate the group! If you are aware that you are saying a lot, make space for others to contribute. Be sensitive to other group members and aim to be encouraging. If you disagree with someone, say so but without putting down their contribution.

FOR INDIVIDUALS

▶ Although this book is written with a group in mind, it can also be easily used by individuals. You obviously won't be able to do the group activities suggested, but you can consider how you would answer the questions and write your thoughts in the space provided.

▶ You may find it helpful to talk to a prayer partner about what you have learnt, and ask them to pray for you as you try and apply what you are learning to your life.

INTRODUCTION TO DANIEL

It was the end of life as they knew it. God's chosen people had been taken by force from the Promised Land, from the Holy City, by the most powerful political force of their day. The defeat was crushing; they were numb from shock. On reflection they should have seen it coming - Isaiah, Micah and Jeremiah had warned them punishment would follow if they continued to disobey God. But now, exiled in Babylon with the glory days of Jerusalem and the familiarity of the Jewish way of life a distant memory, hope was fading fast. To the Babylonians, and even to the Israelites in their darker moments, it looked as if Yahweh had been defeated. And even if God was alive how could they serve him in exile? How could they be God's people in a foreign land when all the props their faith relied on had been removed?

The story of Daniel and his three friends showed the Israelites that the exile didn't have to be the end: it could be the beginning. It could be a new opportunity to demonstrate love and obedience to God. It could be the start of a deeper faith which proved God's faithfulness and recognised his sovereignty even in testing times.

The story spans the rule of three kings as we follow Daniel's rise from a young graduate of the Babylonian academy to close confidant of the king, well past retirement age. He excelled in his service to the Babylonians, becoming indispensable to Nebuchadnezzar and later Darius, as an interpreter of dreams and governor of the kingdom. Daniel was an example of an obedient life which God blessed. But working in a pagan culture was not without its problems. The clash between obedience to God and obedience to the State was inevitable. From the day he entered the academy there was pressure to eat food offered to idols, and at the end of his life Daniel was put in the lions' den for praying openly to God. These are the dramatic events recorded in Scripture but the battle to resist the more subtle influences of this pagan culture were constant; the pressure to conform was relentless. But Daniel demonstrated that obedience to God was possible. And for him, what was lost in the exile was more than made up for in renewed intimacy with God.

For believers living in the secular world of the twenty-first century, exiled from our Christian heritage and traditions, Daniel inspires us to hold fast to our faith. His story reminds us that if we offer faithful service to God we will see his faithfulness. Our challenge is to relate to secular society and offer a positive contribution while at the same time preserving the integrity of our faith. Then, perhaps like Daniel, we too will make a difference in the culture and context to which God has called us.

COOPERATION WITHOUT COMPROMISE

AIM: How to relate to contemporary culture without compromising our faith.

Imagine going to a new country with a new culture, new laws, new ways of doing things – not just for a holiday, but for life. That's exactly what the exile meant for the Israelites. They had to learn how to live godly lives in an ungodly environment. In a similar way the twenty-first century church is in exile – Christian values and customs are no longer familiar to our world. In this new context we need to rethink how we practise our faith. How can we have a positive benefit on our society and develop meaningful relationships with those in our community without compromising our fundamental beliefs? How can we make a difference without losing our distinctives?

TO SET THE SCENE
If this is the first time your group has met together, take time to introduce your-selves. Get to know more about each others' lives by sharing an example from your work or home situation where you have had to take a stand for your faith and refuse to compromise your Christian principles. Perhaps there was a decision at work you had to question or an activity you could not take part in. Explain what happened and how other people responded to you.

Read Daniel 1
> *In the third year of the reign of Jehoiakim king of Judah, Nebuchadnezzar king of Babylon came to Jerusalem and besieged it. And the Lord delivered Jehoiakim king of Judah into his hand, along with some of the articles from the temple of God. These he carried off to the temple of his god in Babylonia and put in the treasure house of his god.*
>
> *Then the king ordered Ashpenaz, chief of his court officials, to bring in some of the Israelites from the royal family and the nobility—young men without any physical defect, handsome, showing aptitude for every kind of learning, well informed, quick to understand, and qualified to serve in the king's palace. He was to teach them the language and literature of the Babylonians. The king assigned them a daily amount of food and wine from the king's table. They*

were to be trained for three years, and after that they were to enter the king's service.

Among these were some from Judah: Daniel, Hananiah, Mishael and Azariah. The chief official gave them new names: to Daniel, the name Belteshazzar; to Hananiah, Shadrach; to Mishael, Meshach; and to Azariah, Abednego.

But Daniel resolved not to defile himself with the royal food and wine, and he asked the chief official for permission not to defile himself this way. Now God had caused the official to show favour and sympathy to Daniel, but the official told Daniel, "I am afraid of my lord the king, who has assigned your food and drink. Why should he see you looking worse than the other young men your age? The king would then have my head because of you."

Daniel then said to the guard whom the chief official had appointed over Daniel, Hananiah, Mishael and Azariah, "Please test your servants for ten days: Give us nothing but vegetables to eat and water to drink. Then compare our appearance with that of the young men who eat the royal food, and treat your servants in accordance with what you see." So he agreed to this and tested them for ten days.

At the end of the ten days they looked healthier and better nourished than any of the young men who ate the royal food. So the guard took away their choice food and the wine they were to drink and gave them vegetables instead.

To these four young men God gave knowledge and understanding of all kinds of literature and learning. And Daniel could understand visions and dreams of all kinds.

At the end of the time set by the king to bring them in, the chief official pre-sented them to Nebuchadnezzar. The king talked with them, and he found none equal to Daniel, Hananiah, Mishael and Azariah; so they entered the king's service. In every matter of wisdom and understanding about which the king questioned them, he found them ten times better than all the magicians and enchanters in his whole kingdom.

And Daniel remained there until the first year of King Cyrus.

Daniel 1

WHAT DOES SEARCH THE BIBLE SAY? **1.** Some Babylonians and even some Israelites may have thought that the exile meant God had been defeated. What evidence is there in chapter 1 that God is alive and orchestrating events?

2. Why did God allow the Israelites to be carried off into exile? See 2 Chronicles 36:14–21.

3. How would life be different for the Israelites living in exile? In particular, what places, structures, and aspects of Jewish culture would they miss in Babylon?

4. In what ways did Daniel and his friends cooperate with the foreign regime?

5. Why do you think Daniel refused to compromise when it came to eating the food and wine from the king's table? Why was this issue more important than accepting foreign names?

> *As Christians enter the twenty-first century, they do so as exiles, strangers and pilgrims, aliens in a strange land. They will need to learn the strategies of survival, and to sing the songs of Zion in the midst of Babylon.*
>
> **Kenneth Leech**

HOW DOES THIS APPLY **6.** As a Christian to what extent do you identify with the term 'resident alien' (Hebrews 11:13, 1 Peter 1:1, 2:11)? To what extent do you consider yourself living in exile?

7. Like Daniel we are commanded to live godly lives in an ungodly society. Where would you draw the boundary lines? Discuss how you would react in the following scenarios.
- A girl in your daughter's class is going to the cinema for her 12th birthday party and your

daughter has been invited. The group is going to see a film with a 15 certificate. Another Christian parent is allowing her child to go. What do you do?

- A young man in your house group is involved in local government. He explains that it would be counter-productive to promote his Christian principles on every issue at work. Another member of the group feels he should stand up for his Christian principles at all times. How could you help resolve this disagreement and what issues would you encourage him to take a stand on?
- Your son enjoys sport and is regularly picked to play on the school's football team. Unfortunately, a lot of the matches are played on Sundays. Would you allow him to play, acknowledging that this is just a phase, and believing that God would want him to use his gifts; would you refuse saying you want to keep Sunday special; or would you come to some sort of compromise?

8. Jeremiah told the exiles to 'seek the peace and prosperity of the city' (Jer. 29:4–7). What is your church doing to 'seek the peace and prosperity' of the community? Can this be done without compromising the fundamentals of faith?

9. What lessons do you think Daniel and his friends learnt about God while they were in exile? Were there any lessons they learnt in Babylon that they could not have learnt at home?

10. What have you learnt about God and about yourself
- in times of loss, when God has taken away what was familiar to you;
- in times when you have taken a stand, refusing to compromise your Christian principles?

Daniel and his friends ... were fully immersed in a pagan culture. They worked hard and succeeded in society. But they did not compromise their religious principles. They challenge the position of those who say it is impossible to be totally committed to God and his principles in a fallen world.

Ajith Fernando

WORSHIP

Spend time quietly reflecting on what God has taught you from Daniel chapter 1.

▶ Perhaps you feel abandoned by God and in spiritual exile. Ask God what he wants you to learn in this difficult season of life.

▶ Perhaps you need to repent for an occasion you compromised your Christian principles and let God down.

▶ Perhaps you need to ask for God's strength to take a stand on a particular issue at home or at work.

If it is appropriate, share these particular issues with another member of the group. As you pray for each other put your hand on the other person's shoulder to symbolise that whatever is going on in your lives, and however far away God may feel, he has his hand on your life, he is in control and has a plan.

Close your session together by singing songs of praise to God thanking him for his power, sovereignty and faithfulness in your life.

BOOKS TO READ

New Issues Facing Christians Today by John Stott (Zondervan, 2005) will help you explore further how Christians should interact with contemporary society.

Invading Secular Space: Strategies for Tomorrow's Church by Martin Robinson and Dwight Smith (Monarch, 2003) addresses how the local church can influence and be a force for good in our post-Christian society.

DURING THE WEEK

Ask God to show you where to draw the boundaries lines in your work and home situation. Listen for his reply and look for opportunities to demonstrate your faith in a winsome way. Don't compare yourself to anyone else! Notice that Daniel didn't seek approval from his friends before he decided not to eat food from the king's table – he made his own decision regardless of who would follow him or the consequences.

Session 2 looks at Daniel chapter 2 which is a long chapter. If you have time during the week, it would be good to read this chapter.

ULTIMATE TRIUMPH

AIM

Aim: To consider how we should live given God's ultimate triumph over evil.

How many times have you heard someone say, 'If only I'd known...'? So often we would have acted differently in a situation if we'd known the big picture. Biblical prophecies give us the big picture perspective on Christianity and assure us Christ will triumph. So what difference does this make? What difference should Christ's ultimate triumph over evil make to how we react to our present difficulties, how we face our anxieties and how we interact with the world?

TO SET THE SCENE

Daniel explained to the king, 'There is a God in heaven who reveals mysteries' (2:28). In what ways does God reveal mysteries today? Brainstorm all the different ways God uses to reveal his truth to individuals and to the church. Ask if any members of the group would like to share ways God has spoken to them.

Read Daniel 2:1-3, 24-49

In the second year of his reign, Nebuchadnezzar had dreams; his mind was troubled and he could not sleep. So the king summoned the magicians, enchanters, sorcerers and astrologers to tell him what he had dreamed. When they came in and stood before the king, he said to them, "I have had a dream that troubles me and I want to know what it means."

Daniel 2:1-3

Then Daniel went to Arioch, whom the king had appointed to execute the wise men of Babylon, and said to him, "Do not execute the wise men of Babylon. Take me to the king, and I will interpret his dream for him."

Arioch took Daniel to the king at once and said, "I have found a man among the exiles from Judah who can tell the king what his dream means."

The king asked Daniel (also called Belteshazzar), "Are you able to tell me what I saw in my dream and interpret it?"

Daniel replied, "No wise man, enchanter, magician or diviner can explain to the king the mystery he has asked about, but there is a God in heaven who reveals mysteries. He has shown King Nebuchadnezzar what will happen in days to come. Your dream and the visions that passed through your mind as you lay on your bed are these:

"As you were lying there, O king, your mind turned to things to come, and the revealer of mysteries showed you what is going to happen. As for me, this mystery has been revealed to me, not because I have greater wisdom than other living men, but so that you, O king, may know the interpretation and that you may understand what went through your mind.

"You looked, O king, and there before you stood a large statue—an enormous, dazzling statue, awesome in appearance. The head of the statue was made of pure gold, its chest and arms of silver, its belly and thighs of bronze, its legs of iron, its feet partly of iron and partly of baked clay. While you were watching, a rock was cut out, but not by human hands. It struck the statue on its feet of iron and clay and smashed them. Then the iron, the clay, the bronze, the silver and the gold were broken to pieces at the same time and became like chaff on a threshing-floor in the summer. The wind swept them away without leaving a trace. But the rock that struck the statue became a huge mountain and filled the whole earth.

"This was the dream, and now we will interpret it to the king. You, O king, are the king of kings. The God of heaven has given you dominion and power and might and glory; in your hands he has placed mankind and the beasts of the field and the birds of the air. Wherever they live, he has made you ruler over them all. You are that head of gold.

"After you, another kingdom will rise, inferior to yours. Next, a third kingdom, one of bronze, will rule over the whole earth. Finally, there will be a fourth kingdom, strong as iron—for iron breaks and smashes everything—and as iron breaks things to pieces, so it will crush and break all the others. Just as you saw that the feet and toes were partly of baked clay and partly of iron, so this will be a divided kingdom; yet it will have some of the strength of iron in it, even as you saw iron mixed with clay. As the toes were partly iron and partly clay, so this kingdom will be partly strong and partly brittle. And just as you saw the iron mixed with baked clay, so the people will be a mixture and will not remain united, any more than iron mixes with clay.

"In the time of those kings, the God of heaven will set up a kingdom that will never be destroyed, nor will it be left to another people. It will crush all those *kingdoms and bring them to an end, but it will itself endure for ever. This is the meaning of the vision of the rock cut out of a mountain, but not by human hands—a rock that broke the iron, the bronze, the clay, the silver and the gold to pieces.*

"The great God has shown the king what will take place in the future. The dream is true and the interpretation is trustworthy."

Then King Nebuchadnezzar fell prostrate before Daniel and paid him honour and ordered that an offering and incense be presented to him. The king said to Daniel, "Surely your God is the God of gods and the Lord of kings and a revealer of mysteries, for you were able to reveal this mystery."

Then the king placed Daniel in a high position and lavished many gifts on him. He made him ruler over the entire province of Babylon and placed him in charge of all its wise men. Moreover, at Daniel's request the king appointed Shadrach, Meshach and Abednego administrators over the province of Babylon, while Daniel himself remained at the royal court.

Daniel 2:24–49

WHAT DOES
SEARCH
THE BIBLE SAY?

1. What are the timeless truths we can learn from Daniel's interpretation of the king's dream?

2. What encouragement do you think the Israelites would have gained from Daniel's prophecy?

3. Look at the parallel vision in chapter 7:9–14, 23–27. What else do we learn about what God's kingdom will be like and who will rule?

4. Daniel's dream foretelling God's ultimate triumph was prophetic.

   a) What was the role of prophecy in the early church? Look at Acts 21:10–11, 1 Thessalonians 5:19–21, 1 Corinthians 14:3, 23–25, 29–33.

   b) What is the role of prophecy in the church today? Ask if any members of the group have received prophetic words from God and how they responded.

Handwritten notes:

Q1. Look to God for wisdom & help. God reveals mysteries. God knows the future. God's king done you never be destroyed. God protects. Give God credit & thanks.

Q2. That God's kingdom is indestructable. That great kings recognise God's power & might.

Q3. God will rule. We will be judged but God but entering God will give his kingdom to his Saints.

Q4 a) Commonly happened & was believed.

b) less common - thought weird?

HOW DOES THIS

APPLY

5. In what ways can the church be a prophetic sign to the world, pointing to the ultimate triumph of good over evil?

Q5. dramatic actions, stand out as different. Being about our beliefs

Christians are not meant to just try and do good, be nice and help the world work a little better. They are intended to act as signposts to another order, another way of life, another kingdom, which can be glimpsed in this world but has not yet arrived completely.

Graham Tomlinson

6. Although he warned the king of the ultimate powerlessness of political empires Daniel served him in the royal court (2:49). To what extent should Christians try to be a prophetic voice in politics? What should our expectations and role be?

7. Despite knowing that good would eventually triumph over evil Daniel was still anxious (7:15, 28). How should we respond to the present evil in the world in the light of God's ultimate triumph?

8. If the kingdom of God will ultimately triumph what value and significance does this bring to our daily work and ministry?

9. How will the message behind Daniel's dreams make a difference to you this week?

WORSHIP
Close your eyes as a member of the group reads Daniel 7:9–14 – the prophecy foretelling God's ultimate triumph. Try and imagine the scene. Share your impressions of the court scene with the group and use the thoughts, encouragements and challenges this scene provokes to lead you into a time of worship. Spend time praising God for who he is, what he has done and what he promises to do. Then in twos pray for each other's present struggles and concerns – pray that you will respond in the light of God's ultimate triumph.

BOOKS TO READ
If you'd like to investigate the role of prophecy in the church today a good starting point is the *The Prophetic Imagination* by Walter Brueggemann (Augsburg, 2001).

You may like to look in more depth at possible interpretations for the empires mentioned in Daniel's dream. Useful commentaries are *The Message of Daniel* by Ronald Wallace (IVP, 1984) and *The Expositor's Bible Commentary Volume 7* edited by Frank Gaebelein (Zondervan, 1985).

DURING THE WEEK
Despite trusting in God's ultimate triumph over evil we may still face heartache, struggles and tough decisions this week. Keep your focus on God by remembering that whatever your situation, 'There is a God in heaven...' (2:28).

ACTIVITY PAGE

Authentic Christianity is not learning a set of doctrines and then stepping out into cadence with people all marching the same way. It is not simply humanitarian service to the less fortunate. It is a walk, a supernatural walk with a living, dynamic, communicating God. Thus the heart and soul of the Christian life is learning to hear God's voice and developing the courage to do what he tells us to do.

Bill Hybels

Daniel's prayer in 2:17–23 is a good example of how to pray.

▶ It is good to pray with others (Matt. 18:19–20).
▶ We should thank God in advance for working in our situation – Daniel thanked God for revealing the interpretation to the dream before he'd checked with the king it was right!
▶ We need to acknowledge God's greatness and sovereign control.
▶ We need to acknowledge that all we are and have comes from God.

Follow Daniel's lead and organise a specific prayer time for your group. The following are some practical suggestions to help you get started.

▶ Decide a time when you can get together and pray – perhaps a Saturday morning or an evening during the week or devote a whole house group meeting to prayer.
▶ Decide in advance what specific issues you are going to pray about.
▶ Discuss together if you want to fast as well.
▶ Begin by praising God – perhaps use Daniel's prayer or other Scripture verses to help you focus on who God is.
▶ Have worship tapes and CDs available.
▶ Intersperse your prayers with Scripture readings and songs.
▶ Introduce variety - move around as you pray, stand, kneel or sit. Pray on your own, in twos and as a larger group.
▶ Include silence. Listen to what God is saying to you and be prepared to align your will to his.
▶ After your time together evaluate how the session went and what you could improve.

If you would like more ideas for your prayer session read one of the books below for inspiration.

The Power of a Praying Wife (Kingsway, 2001), *The Power of a Praying Husband* (Harvest House, 2001) and *The Power of a Praying Parent* (Kingsway, 2000) all by Stormie O'Martian. Very practical books on praying for family members.

Red Moon Rising by Pete Greig and Dave Roberts (Relevant Books, 2003) tells the challenging story of the 24-7 prayer movement.

Bill Hybel's *Too Busy Not to Pray* (IVP, 1998) has become a classic book on prayer.

FAITH UNDER FIRE

AIM

Aim: To consider God's role and our response to persecution

In the film *The Matrix* Morpheus says to Neo 'Sooner or later you're going to realise that there's a difference between knowing the path and walking the path.' That's also true for Christians – sooner or later there comes a point when we realise the difference between knowing the truth and living it. When struggles and persecution come and we choose to live out our faith there's an opportunity for unique spiritual growth as we see God's faithfulness and he sees ours.

TO SET THE SCENE *self centred* *Psalm 137; 57*

Nebuchadnezzar built the statue to promote a common religion that would unite society. What is the common 'religion' of our day? What are the beliefs we are all supposed to adhere to? Brainstorm together the top ten ideas that are promoted as 'non-negotiable' and intended to bind our society together. It might help to look at magazines and newspapers to see the values promoted by the media. *social bound*

nous culture *Celebrity – materialism, summing, football bl* *guidelines* *values promoted by media*

Read Daniel 3:1–18

> *King Nebuchadnezzar made an image of gold, ninety feet high and nine feet wide, and set it up on the plain of Dura in the province of Babylon. He then summoned the satraps, prefects, governors, advisers, treasurers, judges, magistrates and all the other provincial officials to come to the dedication of the image he had set up. So the satraps, prefects, governors, advisers, treasurers, judges, magistrates and all the other provincial officials assembled for the dedication of the image that King Nebuchadnezzar had set up, and they stood before it.*
>
> *Then the herald loudly proclaimed, "This is what you are commanded to do, O peoples, nations and men of every language: As soon as you hear the sound of the horn, flute, zither, lyre, harp, pipes and all kinds of music, you must fall down and worship the image of gold that King Nebuchadnezzar has set up. Whoever does not fall down and worship will immediately be thrown into a blazing furnace." Therefore, as soon as they heard the sound of the horn, flute, zither, lyre, harp and all kinds of music, all the peoples, nations and men of*

every language fell down and worshipped the image of gold that King Neb-uchadnezzar had set up.

At this time some astrologers came forward and denounced the Jews. They said to King Nebuchadnezzar, "O king, live forever! You have issued a decree, O king, that everyone who hears the sound of the horn, flute, zither, lyre, harp, pipes and all kinds of music must fall down and worship the image of gold, and that whoever does not fall down and worship will be thrown into a blazing furnace. But there are some Jews whom you have set over the affairs of the province of Babylon—Shadrach, Meshach and Abednego—who pay no attention to you, O king. They neither serve your gods nor worship the image of gold you have set up."

Furious with rage, Nebuchadnezzar summoned Shadrach, Meshach and Abednego. So these men were brought before the king, and Nebuchadnezzar said to them, "Is it true, Shadrach, Meshach and Abednego, that you do not serve my gods or worship the image of gold I have set up? Now when you hear the sound of the horn, flute, zither, lyre, harp, pipes and all kinds of music, if you are ready to fall down and worship the image I made, very good. But if you do not worship it, you will be thrown immediately into a blazing furnace. Then what god will be able to rescue you from my hand?"

Shadrach, Meshach and Abednego replied to the king, "O Nebuchadnezzar, we do not need to defend ourselves before you in this matter. If we are thrown into the blazing furnace, the God we serve is able to save us from it, and he will rescue us from your hand, O king. But even if he does not, we want you to know, O king, that we will not serve your gods or worship the image of gold you have set up."

Daniel 3:1–18

1. What factors do you think played a part in the three friends' decision not to bow down before the golden idol? 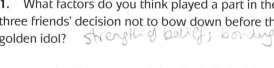 *strength of belief; bonding.*

 *prepared to take, not for God, despite consequences*

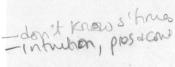 *don't know s'times - intuition, pros & cons*

HOW DOES THIS
?
APPLY
2. The men didn't justify their decision but simply said, 'We do not need to defend ourselves before you in this matter' (3:16). How do we know when it is appropriate to explain ourselves and when it is best to keep silent? What advice would you give in the following scenarios:

- A Christian biology teacher decided to promote creationism rather than Darwinism in his classes. He did not speak to his head of department about his decision and now faces a backlash from parents and other teachers – what should he do? *explain himself*

  apologise, keep quiet
  teach the curriculum
  offer alternative - give child a choice

- It is usual for the people in your office to inflate their expense claims each month. You do not and your boss publicly praises you for your thriftiness in front of all your colleagues. How should you handle the matter with your colleagues now?

  explain why you don't inflate exp
  keep silent unless asked by colleague

- You are married to a non-Christian but want to put money in the church collection each Sunday. Should you discuss your plans with your spouse and only go ahead if they consent; should you take the money out of your own monthly allowance; or just not mention anything and hope he doesn't notice?

  try discussing the job"

WHAT DOES SEARCH THE BIBLE SAY? **3.** What details does the author cite to emphasise how amazing it was that the three men survived the furnace? Look at verses 19–23.

the strength of the soldiers
the tying up
the heat
death of soldiers

4. God wanted to teach Nebuchadnezzar a lesson about how powerful he was. What lesson do you think he wanted to teach the three friends?

that sticking together was good
+ trust in God is repaid

> *A faith that is based on good people thanking God because they've prospered has no answers at all in the face of an Exile.*
>
> **John Holdsworth**

5. What lessons can we learn through persecution if we are willing? Look at Job 2:3, 2 Corinthians 12:7–10, Hebrews 12:4–12, 1 Peter 1:6–9.

God sends us trials or trib to show us he can look after us if we trust in him, persecution but trust god

6. Share examples of what God has taught you through difficult times? If appropriate, have a time of prayer reflecting on God's faithfulness in times of difficulty.

shake of faith
prayer (power) mor
trust in him
footprints in sand'

When I was beaten on the bottom of my feet, my tongue cried. Why did my tongue cry? It was not beaten. It cried because the tongue and feet are both part of the same body. And you free Christians are part of the same body of Christ that is now beaten in prisons, restricted nations, that even now gives martyrs for Christ. Can you not feel our pain?

Richard Wurmbrand

7. How would you reply to Richard Wurmbrand's question? What is your church doing to help those being persecuted? Is there more you could do?

8. How would you respond to someone who said, 'Christians in Britain are being persecuted – we are portrayed negatively in the media, it is not politically correct to share our beliefs, and almost any other religion is tolerated more than Christianity – unfortunately most of us are too comfortable to notice what is happening.' Do you agree with this statement?

WORSHIP

Quietly think through some of the issues raised in this chapter.

▶ Daniel's friends were willing to die because they wanted to worship God alone. What has your worship cost you this week?

▶ The friends objected to worshipping another god. What other gods have we allowed to consume our attention this week?

▶ The friends knew God could rescue them, but they said to the king, 'But even if he (God) does not ... we will not serve your gods or worship the image' (3:18). Consider the matters you are praying about. Ask God to enable you to say, 'But even if he does not...'

BOOKS TO READ

Our faith is often challenged when we read the stories of others, especially those who have persevered through hardship and persecution. Go to your local Christian bookshop and choose a biography to read. *The Heavenly Man* by Brother Yun (Monarch, 2002) is an inspiring account of one man's experience of God in communist China.

DURING THE WEEK

As you face pressures and challenges to your faith this week imagine the fourth man − the pre-incarnate Christ − physically present, walking alongside you. Draw strength from his presence, his example and his prayers on your behalf.

ACTIVITY PAGE

Confidence born out of belief empowers those who might otherwise cower in fear to engage boldly with the idols and idolatry of their age. The faith that thrives in the exile of the 21st century will be a faith that is fully and resiliently engaged with the culture in which it is set.

Gerard Kelly

The following is a list of some of the idols in our age and culture.

TOLERANCE
INDEPENDENCE
INDIVIDUALITY
POWER
IMAGE
SEX
MONEY
PLEASURE
FREEDOM

▶ Rank these idols in order of prominence and influence in society.
▶ How have you seen these idols express themselves? Think for example:
   a) How does our society demonstrate it makes a god of image/tolerance/ pleasure etc
   b) Look through the magazines and newspapers from the To Set the Scene exercise to find examples of these idols in our everyday lives.
▶ Which of these idols are seen in the church? Give specific examples of how image/individuality/independence etc are expressed in the church.
▶ How can the church address these contemporary issues without making idols of them?
▶ What other idols do you think we have?

HEAVEN RULES

AIM

Aim: To acknowledge God's rule in our lives as well as the world

As children, teenagers and adults we strive for independence. Local communities and even family relationships break down as we all long to 'do it our own way'. In our spiritual lives too it's easy to lose focus on God and start believing that we're responsible for our own success and status in life. Instead of thinking like God we start to think we are God!

TO SET THE SCENE
How do you think your friends, neighbours and work colleagues would answer the question: 'Who controls your life'? What game would best fit their answer?

▶ Snakes and Ladders – ultimately fate controls my destiny.
▶ Chess – I need to plan ahead and make wise decisions because life is what I make it.
▶ Grab – my bank manager, employer, and spouse all have more control over my life than I do.
▶ Monopoly – creating wealth and acquiring possessions gives me control of my life and other people's.

What game best reflects different stages of your life?

Read Daniel 4:1–8, 24–37
King Nebuchadnezzar,

To the peoples, nations and men of every language, who live in all the world:

May you prosper greatly!

It is my pleasure to tell you about the miraculous signs and wonders that the Most High God has performed for me.

How great are his signs, how mighty his wonders! His kingdom is an eternal kingdom; his dominion endures from generation to generation.

I, Nebuchadnezzar, was at home in my palace, contented and prosperous. I had a dream that made me afraid. As I was lying in my bed, the images and visions that passed through my mind terrified me. So I commanded that all the wise men of Babylon be brought before me to interpret the dream for me. When the magicians, enchanters, astrologers and diviners came, I told them the dream, but they could not interpret it for me. Finally, Daniel came into my presence and I told him the dream. (He is called Belteshazzar, after the name of my god, and the spirit of the holy gods is in him.)

Daniel 4:1−8

"This is the interpretation, O king, and this is the decree the Most High has issued against my lord the king: You will be driven away from people and will live with the wild animals; you will eat grass like cattle and be drenched with the dew of heaven. Seven times will pass by for you until you acknowledge that the Most High is sovereign over the kingdoms of men and gives them to anyone he wishes. The command to leave the stump of the tree with its roots means that your kingdom will be restored to you when you acknowledge that Heaven rules. Therefore, O king, be pleased to accept my advice: Renounce your sins by doing what is right, and your wickedness by being kind to the oppressed. It may be that then your prosperity will continue.

All this happened to King Nebuchadnezzar. Twelve months later, as the king was walking on the roof of the royal palace of Babylon, he said, "Is not this the great Babylon I have built as the royal residence, by my mighty power and for the glory of my majesty?"

The words were still on his lips when a voice came from heaven, "This is what is decreed for you, King Nebuchadnezzar: Your royal authority has been taken from you. You will be driven away from people and will live with the wild animals; you will eat grass like cattle. Seven times will pass by for you until you acknowledge that the Most High is sovereign over the kingdoms of men and gives them to anyone he wishes."

Immediately what had been said about Nebuchadnezzar was fulfilled. He was driven away from people and ate grass like cattle. His body was drenched with the dew of heaven until his hair grew like the feathers of an eagle and his nails like the claws of a bird.

At the end of that time, I, Nebuchadnezzar, raised my eyes towards heaven, and my sanity was restored. Then I praised the Most High; I honoured and glorified him who lives for ever.

His dominion is an eternal dominion; his kingdom endures from generation to generation.

All the peoples of the earth are regarded as nothing. He does as he pleases with the powers of heaven and the peoples of the earth. No-one can hold back his hand or say to him: "What have you done?"

At the same time that my sanity was restored, my honour and splendour were returned to me for the glory of my kingdom. My advisers and nobles sought me out, and I was restored to my throne and became even greater than before. Now I, Nebuchadnezzar, praise and exalt and glorify the King of heaven, because everything he does is right and all his ways are just. And those who walk in pride he is able to humble.

Daniel 4:24–37

WHAT DOES
SEARCH
THE BIBLE SAY?

1. Retrace Nebuchadnezzar's response to God. Look at Daniel 2:46–49, 3:28–30, 4: 28–37. How did his response change over time? What was the reason for it?

— humbled as was once g ther sad/made etc
Personal experience

2. Nebuchadnezzar eventually learnt the key lesson that 'the Most High is sovereign over the kingdoms of men and gives them to anyone he wishes and sets over them the lowliest of men' (4:17). How does this truth help you think about modern politics, dictators and terrorist threats?

Nelson Mandela

3. What authority do you exercise? What difference does it make knowing God has given you this position of authority?

with grace

In family overthe d
In career
feel braver to talk about faith.

4. How can we reconcile the idea that 'heaven rules' over the affairs of earth now (4:26) and Jesus' command to pray, 'Your will be done on earth as it is in heaven' (Matt. 6:10)? Is God in control or not?

— we have free will but should pray to God a little
it should be a partnership btwn us & him

5. Look at the last few verses of each of the first six chapters of Daniel. How was God teaching the Israelites about his sovereign control and faithfulness?

6. What circumstances, events or people has God used to teach you about his sovereignty?

[handwritten: Work, family children, home]

7. The king was proud of his achievements and said, 'Is not this the great Babylon I have built as the royal residence, by my mighty power and for the glory of my majesty?' Be honest. What is your Babylon? What are the achievements and accomplishments you are proud of and that give you a sense of security?

[handwritten: My personal faith home grp. Sunday Grp weight loss]

8. What lessons can we learn from Daniel 4 about

- how we should view our achievements? Refer to specific verses.
- how God views human achievements? (Look at 4:26, 36–37.)

[handwritten: they are by the grace of God don't let ur achievements cause us 2 4get God ok if supporting mankind]

9. What habits and practices can we put in place to keep a right perspective on God's achievements and our own?

[handwritten: Praise him for his achievements & thank him 4 ours use his gifts to us for his glory. Give wealth etc use talents]

> *I often hear Christian leaders tell what God has been saying to them in their times of meditation and study and prayer and I'm often amazed. He tells them the most profound, eloquent things. All I seem to ever hear is: 'Rob, get out of the way.'*
>
> **Rob Bell**

WORSHIP

Notice that chapter 4 opens and closes with praising God (4:3, 34–37). Try beginning and ending your time together by praising God.

> At the beginning of the session choose songs and prayers that help you focus on God's greatness and put your own problems to one side.
> At the end of your session follow Nebuchadnezzar's example and declare to one another the attributes of God that you are thankful for.
> Notice in 4:37 the king says, 'I praise and exalt the king of heaven, because everything he does is right and all his ways are just.' You may struggle with this statement about God. Perhaps you feel he has not dealt rightly or justly with your concerns. Pray in twos that God would help you see that even in your situation 'heaven rules'.

BOOKS TO READ

If you want to think through some of the key issues related to how Christians deal with wealth, success and status, then take a look at the series of books written by Neil Hood (published by Authentic).

Whose Life Is It Anyway? A Lifeline in a Stress-Soaked World
God's Payroll: Whose Work Is It Anyway?
God's Wealth: Whose Money Is It Anyway?

DURING THE WEEK

This week look for opportunities to demonstrate your dependence on God rather than your money, status or achievements. Give a generous gift into the offering on Sunday or to a particular individual in need; at work take time to pray before giving presentations or meeting clients; when you meet new people at church pray God would give you words to encourage them rather than using the conversation to explain your own job, role or position.

ACTIVITY PAGE

'It is my pleasure to tell you about the miraculous signs and wonders that the Most High God has performed for me.' (4:2)

Daniel 4 was an open letter written by King Nebuchadnezzar to his people telling them about his personal encounter with God and how his life changed as a result. You might like to try writing a 'Nebuchadnezzar letter'. Think back as far as you can remember and then record all the ways God has been active in your life. Write down all his blessings, the ways he has intervened at special times, how he has comforted you in difficulties and encouraged you to grow as a Christian.

Do you see any pattern in the way God has been working in your life? Any particular group of people he keeps bringing to your attention, any ministry you feel particularly drawn to or any gifts he keeps giving you the opportunity to develop? Reflect on the key ways God has worked in your life and see if this helps you discern where he might be leading you now.

If it is appropriate you could share your letter and any issues it raises with the group.

A PLAY FOR POWER

AIM: To recognise God's power at work in our lives and in the world

When people know the outcome of something they often talk of 'the writing being on the wall'. In our spiritual lives we long to know for sure that God is at work, to hear his voice clearly, to see his power displayed dramatically. In other words we want to see 'the writing on the wall'. And yet if we look more closely God is continually demonstrating his power. Maybe he doesn't write on walls these days, but he still colours the sky at sunset, speaks through human voices and touches people's hearts. Perhaps the problem is not that God has stopped demonstrating his power but that we've stopped recognising it.

TO SET THE SCENE
Brainstorm all the different ways you have seen God show his power including

▶ The most recent time you saw God demonstrating his power.
▶ The most impressive display of God's power you've ever seen.
▶ The time you didn't realise God's power was at work until much later.

Read Daniel 5

King Belshazzar gave a great banquet for a thousand of his nobles and drank wine with them. While Belshazzar was drinking his wine, he gave orders to bring in the gold and silver goblets that Nebuchadnezzar his father had taken from the temple in Jerusalem, so that the king and his nobles, his wives and his concubines might drink from them. So they brought in the gold goblets that had been taken from the temple of God in Jerusalem, and the king and his nobles, his wives and his concubines drank from them. As they drank the wine, they praised the gods of gold and silver, of bronze, iron, wood and stone.

Suddenly the fingers of a human hand appeared and wrote on the plaster of the wall, near the lampstand in the royal palace. The king watched the hand as it wrote. His face turned pale and he was so frightened that his knees knocked together and his legs gave way.

The king called out for the enchanters, astrologers and diviners to be brought and said to these wise men of Babylon, "Whoever reads this writing and tells me what it means will be clothed in purple and have a gold chain placed around his neck, and he will be made the third highest ruler in the kingdom."

Then all the king's wise men came in, but they could not read the writing or tell the king what it meant. So King Belshazzar became even more terrified and his face grew more pale. His nobles were baffled.

The queen, hearing the voices of the king and his nobles, came into the banquet hall. "O king, live for ever!" she said. "Don't be alarmed! Don't look so pale! There is a man in your kingdom who has the spirit of the holy gods in him. In the time of your father he was found to have insight and intelligence and wisdom like that of the gods. King Nebuchadnezzar your father—your father the king, I say—appointed him chief of the magicians, enchanters, astrologers and diviners. This man Daniel, whom the king called Belteshazzar, was found to have a keen mind and knowledge and understanding, and also the ability to interpret dreams, explain riddles and solve difficult problems. Call for Daniel, and he will tell you what the writing means."

So Daniel was brought before the king, and the king said to him, "Are you Daniel, one of the exiles my father the king brought from Judah? I have heard that the spirit of the gods is in you and that you have insight, intelligence and outstanding wisdom. The wise men and enchanters were brought before me to read this writing and tell me what it means, but they could not explain it. Now I have heard that you are able to give interpretations and to solve difficult problems. If you can read this writing and tell me what it means, you will be clothed in purple and have a gold chain placed around your neck, and you will be made the third highest ruler in the kingdom."

Then Daniel answered the king, "You may keep your gifts for yourself and give your rewards to someone else. Nevertheless, I will read the writing for the king and tell him what it means.

"O king, the Most High God gave your father Nebuchadnezzar sovereignty and greatness and glory and splendour. Because of the high position he gave him, all the peoples and nations and men of every language dreaded and feared him. Those the king wanted to put to death, he put to death; those he wanted to spare, he spared; those he wanted to promote, he promoted; and those he wanted to humble, he humbled. But when his heart became arrogant and hardened with pride, he was deposed from his royal throne and stripped of his glory. He was driven away from people and given the mind of an animal; he lived with the wild donkeys and ate grass like cattle; and his body was drenched with the dew of heaven, until he acknowledged that the Most High God is sovereign over the kingdoms of men and sets over them anyone he wishes.

"But you his son, O Belshazzar, have not humbled yourself, though you knew all this. Instead, you have set yourself up against the Lord of heaven. You had the goblets from his temple brought to you, and you and your nobles, your wives and your concubines drank wine from them. You praised the gods of silver and gold, of bronze, iron, wood and stone, which cannot see or hear or understand. But you did not honour the God who holds in his hand your life and all your ways. Therefore he sent the hand that wrote the inscription.

"This is the inscription that was written:

MENE, MENE, TEKEL, PARSIN

"This is what these words mean:

Mene: God has numbered the days of your reign and brought it to an end.
Tekel: You have been weighed on the scales and found wanting.
Peres: Your kingdom is divided and given to the Medes and Persians."

Then at Belshazzar's command, Daniel was clothed in purple, a gold chain was placed around his neck, and he was proclaimed the third highest ruler in the kingdom.

That very night Belshazzar, king of the Babylonians, was slain, and Darius the Mede took over the kingdom, at the age of sixty-two.

Daniel 5

WHAT DOES SEARCH THE BIBLE SAY?   **1.** It is obvious that a number of years had passed between the end of chapter 4 and the beginning of chapter 5. Why do you think the author deliberately missed out this detail in order to put these two accounts back-to-back?

2. How can you account for God's apparently different treatment of Nebuchadnezzar and Belshazzar?

3. Look at 5:22–23. What are the specific sins Belshazzar is accused of? What was particularly abhorrent about these sins?

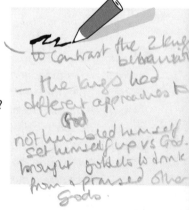

HOW DOES THIS
APPLY

4. In what ways does our society influence us to treat God and what he calls 'holy' lightly?

5. a) Brainstorm ways in which our post-Christian society attempts to challenge the power of God.

b) Are the following practices examples of power entrusted to us by God or are they attempts to usurp God's power?

- IVF treatment
- Human embryo cloning

6. Do you think the modern church needs to recover a sense of the power of God? If so, how?

In a world where many leaders are focused on their own self-enhancement, projected image and drive to control, Jesus teaches us another way. It is a way of being powerful when you are weak, tough when you are soft and huge when you are small. It is absolutely subversive of the model given to us by a self-besotted world.

Viv Thomas

7. Why do you think Christians fail to fully rely on the power of God?

8. If it is appropriate, in twos share where you need to see the power of God in your life. Pray together about these issues.

God's power may come in the form of wisdom, an idea you desperately need and can't come up with yourself. It may come in the form of greater courage than you could ever muster. It may come in the form of confidence or perseverance, uncommon staying power, a changed attitude towards a spouse or child or parent, changed circumstances, maybe even outright miracles. However it comes, God's power is released in the lives of people who pray.

Jim Cymbala

Handwritten notes:

④ swearing, religion less 'sense', no sense of duty/honour. materialism creeps in. Sunday not sacred. no 'fear' of God.

⑤ We are not punished if break 10 C's so have no 'fear' & respect. God alone independance attitude. Teaching as children not serious

See good example from church leaders.

too self centred. / scared? How would it change our way of living if we did? Don't pray enough & listen to God

WORSHIP

Take time to repent of the ways in which we are like Belshazzar. Is there a sense in which God could say to us:

> 'You have not humbled yourself' (5:22).
> 'You have set yourself up against the Lord of heaven' (5:23).
> 'You did not honour the God who holds in his hand your life and all your ways' (5:23).

After you have examined your own heart and repented you may like to share communion with each other. The bread and wine point us back to Calvary for at the cross we see:

> God's unmistakable power demonstrated in the forgiveness of sins.
> Jesus' power seen through weakness and in his submission to his Father.

As you consider the coming week pray together that you would depend on God's power and that you would follow Jesus' example when you exercise power.

BOOKS TO READ

Fresh Power by Jim Cymbala (Zondervan, 2001) recounts the remarkable story of God's work in the Brooklyn Tabernacle in New York. By introducing us to the lives of transformed individuals the author challenges us to a radical dependence on God's power.

DURING THE WEEK

Unlike Nebuchadnezzar there is no evidence that Belshazzar showed any positive response to the word of God he heard from Daniel. Consider how you are responding to the word of God. Does what you hear on a Sunday and what you read in your private devotions make a difference to your daily life? Are there practical measures you could take so that you are more ready to respond to God? Consider what measures you could take:

> Before you go to church
> While you are in church
> During the week

ACTIVITY PAGE

Many people say 'no' to God. Some like Nebuchadnezzar are won round slowly; others like Belshazzar seem to have a blatant disregard for God. In either case what is our responsibility? How do we share the gospel in our homes and workplaces when people are hostile to God? Consider how you would respond in the following scenarios:

▶ Your friend is distressed because her elderly father, who doesn't have long to live, has rejected God. What would be appropriate to say to her?
▶ The minister is concerned about the growing number of women with unsaved husbands who are attending your church. He asks for your help. What practical ideas could you come up with to care for and support these women?
▶ You've told people at work you go to church, you've promoted Christian values in discussions and you've explained why you're a Christian to a few of your colleagues. But no one has shown any interest in your subtle attempts at evangelism. What should you do next? How can you take things further?

If it is appropriate you could explain to the group relationships in your own life where people are hostile to God. Perhaps your spouse, family members, or work colleagues are not Christians and at times they make life difficult for you. Other group members may be able to offer some practical advice and pray with you.

TRIED AND TESTED

AIM: To prepare ourselves for a lifetime of faithful service

We cheer the marathon runner on the home stretch because there is something admirable about those who persevere with determination and triumph over the long haul. In the same way there is something admirable about Christians who have proved their faithfulness to God through years of service. Like Daniel these men and women have faced opposition and hardship and developed holy habits to sustain them. Together with the crowd of witnesses in Hebrews these saints urge us to be faithful and to finish the race.

TO SET THE SCENE
Encourage each member of the group to tell the others about an older Christian who has made a big impression on them.

▶ What was it about this believer that impressed you?
▶ In what specific way have they been a role model for you?
▶ What do you think was the key to their spiritual maturity?

Read Daniel 6:1–23

It pleased Darius to appoint 120 satraps to rule throughout the kingdom, with three administrators over them, one of whom was Daniel. The satraps were made accountable to them so that the king might not suffer loss. Now Daniel so distinguished himself among the administrators and the satraps by his exceptional qualities that the king planned to set him over the whole kingdom. At this, the administrators and the satraps tried to find grounds for charges against Daniel in his conduct of government affairs, but they were unable to do so. They could find no corruption in him, because he was trustworthy and neither corrupt nor negligent. Finally these men said, "We will never find any basis for charges against this man Daniel unless it has something to do with the law of his God."

So the administrators and the satraps went as a group to the king and said: "O King Darius, live forever! The royal administrators, prefects, satraps, advisers and governors have all agreed that the king should issue an edict and enforce the decree that anyone who prays to any god or man during the next thirty days, except to you, O king, shall be thrown into the lions' den. Now, O king, issue the decree and put it in writing so that it cannot be altered—in accordance with the laws of the Medes and Persians, which cannot be repealed." So King Darius put the decree in writing.

Now when Daniel learned that the decree had been published, he went home to his upstairs room where the windows opened toward Jerusalem. Three times a day he got down on his knees and prayed, giving thanks to his God, just as he had done before. Then these men went as a group and found Daniel praying and asking God for help. So they went to the king and spoke to him about his royal decree: "Did you not publish a decree that during the next thirty days anyone who prays to any god or man except to you, O king, would be thrown into the lions' den?"

The king answered, "The decree stands—in accordance with the laws of the Medes and Persians, which cannot be repealed."

Then they said to the king, "Daniel, who is one of the exiles from Judah, pays no attention to you, O king, or to the decree you put in writing. He still prays three times a day." When the king heard this, he was greatly distressed; he was determined to rescue Daniel and made every effort until sundown to save him.

Then the men went as a group to the king and said to him, "Remember, O king, that according to the law of the Medes and Persians no decree or edict that the king issues can be changed."

So the king gave the order, and they brought Daniel and threw him into the lions' den. The king said to Daniel, "May your God, whom you serve continually, rescue you!"

A stone was brought and placed over the mouth of the den, and the king sealed it with his own signet ring and with the rings of his nobles, so that Daniel's situation might not be changed. Then the king returned to his palace and spent the night without eating and without any entertainment being brought to him. And he could not sleep.

At the first light of dawn, the king got up and hurried to the lions' den. When he came near the den, he called to Daniel in an anguished voice, "Daniel, servant of the living God, has your God, whom you serve continually, been able to rescue you from the lions?"

Daniel answered, "O king, live forever! My God sent his angel, and he shut the mouths of the lions. They have not hurt me, because I was found innocent in his sight. Nor have I ever done any wrong before you, O king."

The king was overjoyed and gave orders to lift Daniel out of the den. And when Daniel was lifted from the den, no wound was found on him, because he had trusted in his God.

Daniel 6:1–23

WHAT DOES SEARCH THE BIBLE SAY?
1. What three words best describe Daniel's character?

2. Why do you think Daniel's contemporaries disliked him?

3. What can we learn from Daniel's example in this passage and throughout the story about our attitude to work?

4. Once again Daniel had to choose between the government and God. What evidence is there from the passage that Daniel had prepared himself for this decision?

HOW DOES THIS APPLY
5. Daniel is described in 6:4 as 'trustworthy'. What does it mean to be trustworthy in a church context? Discuss what it means to be trustworthy in the following setups:
▶ Explaining the gospel to someone for the first time
▶ Inviting someone to an evangelistic meeting
▶ Talking to someone about their spiritual gifts

6. Has sharing and defending your faith got easier or more difficult as you've grown older? Explain the various factors involved in both cases.

7. Daniel was in his 80s when he faced the lions' den. He had proved his allegiance to God many times so why do you think God allowed him to face yet another trial? Why do you think God allows recurring trials in our lives?

8. What are the challenges and distractions that threaten our allegiance to Christ as we grow older? How can we prepare ourselves to oppose them?

9. As Daniel looked back over his life what do you think he would say about his experience of God? Think through your own life experiences – what has God taught you about himself?

As for you, go on your way till the end. You will rest, and then at the end of the days you will rise to receive your allotted inheritance.
Daniel 12:13

WORSHIP
Meditate on the title 'living God' (6:20). Look at other places in the Bible where this title is used (Deut. 5:26, Josh. 3:10, 1 Sam. 17:26, Jer. 10:10) and declare to each other what this tells us about God.

▶ Thank God for the ways we see him living and active in the book of Daniel.
▶ Thank him for the ways you have seen him living and active in your life.
▶ Bring before him your present concerns and petition him to act as the living God again.
▶ Consider the distractions and temptations you are susceptible to and ask the living God to give you the strength to stay faithful to him for the rest of your life.

On a piece of paper write down what God has taught you from this study and what truths you want to learn to rely on. Keep the piece of paper in your Bible as a reminder of the study and the commitments God has made to you. Close your worship time by singing songs and hymns that focus on the attributes of the living God.

DURING THE WEEK
Daniel was willing to die because he couldn't pray for 30 days! Does prayer matter to us that much? For the next week make a determined effort to have a significant time of prayer each day. Keep a prayer journal to record what you learn and how God answers your prayers. Try not to stop after the week is up – be like Daniel and keep on praying.

At the end of this series of studies review what God has taught you from the story of Daniel.

Share how you have been challenged to:
- Serve your community
- Stand up for Christian principles
- Give prayer a priority
- Get involved in local/national politics
- Focus on God's ultimate triumph rather than your present problems
- Make the most of opportunities to worship
- Have a right perspective on your wealth, status and achievements
- Exercise your power like Christ
- Value what God regards as holy
- Humble yourself before God
- Develop 'holy habits'

Share together the main lessons you have learnt from this study. Are there any ways the group can help you put these lessons into practice? Are there any ways the group can help you keep growing as a Christian?

BOOKS TO READ
Disciplines of a Godly Man by R. Kent Hughes and *Disciplines of a Godly Woman* by Barbara Hughes (Crossway, 2001) give helpful insights as to how we can cultivate holy habits and the spiritual discipline necessary to be faithful to God for the long term.

ACTIVITY PAGE

Daniel's life of service to God is an example of how to grow as a Christian and develop wisdom, maturity, and faithfulness. But Daniel is not our only role model, the church is full of those who have been on the Christian road longer than us, people from whom we can learn and be encouraged.

If you are an older Christian will you help a younger person become established in their faith? If you're a younger Christian are you willing to learn from someone more mature?

Here are some practical ideas to help you grow together as Christians and to learn from each other:

If you're a younger Christian approach an older believer and

▶ Invite them round for a meal to get to know their life story and how they have remained faithful to God.
▶ Ask them to be your prayer partner.
▶ Invite them to give you feedback when you've led a Bible study or been involved in some sort of ministry.
▶ Offer to help them improve their technology skills and text or email them prayer requests!
▶ Watch their lives to see what you can learn from them about hospitality, prayer, giving, for example.

If you're an older Christian approach a younger believer and

▶ Take them with you when you go on a pastoral visit or are involved in some sort of ministry, let them watch how you relate to others and God.
▶ Ask if you could pray for them and be willing to learn about the issues in their life.
▶ Take an interest in their work/home lives.
▶ Organise inter-generational events so that different sections of the church could share each others' lives.
▶ Encourage them by showing in practical ways that you value their input in church ministry.

Brainstorm any other ideas you have and then discuss which ones you will implement.

LEADERS' GUIDE

TO HELP YOU LEAD

You may have led a house group many times before or this may be your first time. Here is some advice on how to lead these studies:

▶ As a group leader, you don't have to be an expert or a lecturer. You are there to facilitate the learning of the group members – helping them to discover for themselves the wisdom in God's word. You should not be doing most of the talking or dishing out the answers, whatever the group expects from you!

▶ You do need to be aware of the group's dynamics, however. People can be quite quick to label themselves and each other in a group situation. One person might be seen as the expert, another the moaner who always has something to complain about. One person may be labelled as quiet and not be expected to contribute; another person may always jump in with something to say. Be aware of the different types of individuals in the group, but don't allow the labels to stick. You may need to encourage those who find it hard to get a word in, and quieten down those who always have something to say. Talk to members between sessions to find out how they feel about the group.

▶ The sessions are planned to try and engage every member in active learning. Of course you cannot force anyone to take part if they don't want to, but it won't be too easy to be a spectator. Activities that ask everyone to write down a word, or talk in twos, and then report back to the group are there for a reason. They give everyone space to think and form their opinion, even if not everyone voices it out loud.

▶ Do adapt the sessions for your group as you feel is appropriate. Some groups may know each other very well and will be prepared to talk at a deep level. New groups may take a bit of time to get to know each other before making themselves vulnerable, but encourage members to share their lives with each other.

▶ You probably won't be able to tackle all the questions in each session so decide in advance which ones are most appropriate to your group and situation.

▶ Encourage a number of replies to each question. The study is not about finding a single right answer, but about sharing experiences and thoughts in order to find out how to apply the Bible to people's lives. When brainstorming, don't be too quick to evaluate the contributions. Write everything down and then have a look to see which suggestions are worth keeping.

▶ Similarly encourage everyone to ask questions, to voice doubts and to discuss difficulties. Some parts of the Bible are difficult to understand. Sometimes the Christian faith throws up paradoxes. Painful things happen to us that make it difficult to see what God is doing. A house group should be a safe place to express all of this. If discussion doesn't resolve the issue, send everyone away to pray about it between sessions, and ask your minister for advice.

- Give yourself time in the week to read through the Bible passage and the questions. Read the Leaders' notes for the session, as different ways of presenting the questions are sometimes suggested. However, during the session don't be too quick to come in with the answer – sometimes people need space to think.
- Delegate as much as you like! The easiest activities to delegate are reading the text, and the worship sessions, but there are other ways to involve the group members. Giving people responsibility can help them own the session much more.
- Pray for group members by name, that God would meet with them during the week. Pray for the group session, for a constructive and helpful time. Ask the Lord to equip you as you lead the group.

THE STRUCTURE OF EACH SESSION

Feedback: find out what people remember from the previous session, or if they have been able to act during the week on what was discussed last time.

To set the scene: an activity or a question to get everyone thinking about the subject to be studied.

Bible reading: it's important to actually read the passage you are studying during the session. Ask someone to prepare this in advance or go around the group reading a verse or two each. Don't assume everyone will be happy to read out loud.

Questions and activities: adapt these as appropriate to your group. Some groups may enjoy a more activity-based approach; some may prefer just to discuss the questions. Try out some new things!

Worship: suggestions for creative worship and prayer are included, which give everyone an opportunity to respond to God, largely individually. Use these alongside singing or other group expressions of worship. Add a prayer time with opportunities to pray for group members and their families and friends.

During the week: this gives a specific task to do during the week, helping people to continue to think about or apply what they have learned.

Books to read: suggestions are given for those people who want to study the themes further.

GROUND RULES

How do people know what is expected of them in a house group situation? Is it ever discussed, or do we just pick up clues for each other? You may find it helpful to discuss some ground rules for the house group at the start of this course, even if your group has been going a long time. This also gives you an opportunity to talk about how you, as the leader, see the group. Ask everyone to think about what they want to get out of the course. How do they want the group to work? What values do they want to be part of the group's experience: honesty, respect, confidentiality? How do they want their contributions to be treated? You could ask everyone to write down three ground rules on slips of paper and put them in a bowl. Pass the bowl around the group. Each person takes out a rule and reads it, and someone collates the list. Discuss the ground rules that have been suggested and come up with a top five. This method enables everyone to contribute fairly anonymously. Alternatively, if your group are all quite vocal, have a straight discussion about it!

SESSION 1

TO SET THE SCENE

Use this exercise to get to know each of the group member's home and work lives better and to show how the message of Daniel is relevant for us today. Don't judge the issues or the ways in which God invites other people to take a stand for him but notice how different Christians draw the boundary lines in different places.

1. The Lord delivered the Israelite king to Nebuchadnezzar; he gave the Babylonians the temple treasures but ensured that they were preserved rather than destroyed (1:2); God caused the official to show favour to Daniel (1:9); God made sure Daniel and his friends looked healthier than the other recruits (1:15); God made the young men excel (1:20); God made sure Daniel had a long tenure, approximately 65 years (1:21).

2. God allowed the Israelites to go into exile because of their unfaithfulness to him, even on the part of the priests. He had warned the people to repent but they had repeatedly ignored him. The exile was discipline – it purified the Israelites (and the land – 2 Chr. 36:21) and refocused their hearts on God.

3. They would miss the city of Jerusalem and the temple where God was worshipped; the laws, courts and all the political structures promoted God's ways with everyone sharing the same values, heritage and social customs; faith in God was assumed rather than challenged; religious festivals galvanised belief and strengthened community ties. The Israelites would miss the familiarity of home and the ease of worshipping the one true God.

4. Daniel and his friends did not appear to resist joining the Babylonian king's academy; they accepted new names associated with foreign gods; they seemed happy to excel and work hard in the new Babylonian regime.

5. They refused the food from the king's table because it had not been prepared according to Mosaic Law and because the first portion was usually offered to idols. The Israelites considered such food contaminated and didn't want to appear to be participating in idol worship. We don't know why Daniel and his friends refused the food but accepted the foreign names. To them the food defiled them in a way that accepting the names did not. Eating the food would have removed their distinctive trait of purity and was simply a boundary line they were not prepared to cross.

6. If your visa states you are a 'resident alien' it means you reside in a foreign country but do not really belong, it is not your permanent home. Allow the group to share their thoughts on the term 'resident alien' and being in exile. Perhaps on some occasions we do feel out of place in the world – when others seem comfortable with blatant immorality for example. But at other times we enjoy all the blessings of living on earth. This is not wrong, perhaps the important principle is the orientation of our hearts, that we stay God-focused rather than being controlled by society's agenda.

7. Encourage people to express their views and discuss the scenarios. Your group may not always agree with each other and prefer to draw the boundary lines in different places but then perhaps some Israelites criticised Daniel for going into the king's academy!

8. Think through what role your church has in the community and what else you could do. Is the church represented on any local boards; do you help out in any community projects; do you run a nursery or coffee shop for local residents; do you have a good relationship with other community groups?

9. Scan through the passage looking for the evidence. No doubt Daniel and his friends would have learnt that God was in control, that he answered their prayers, that he was concerned for his own glory, that he blessed wholehearted obedience, that he was the giver of knowledge and understanding and that he had a plan for the nation of Israel. Perhaps being in Babylon made all their head knowledge about God seem more real – their faith had been tested in a way it could never have been in Jerusalem and God had proved himself faithful.

SESSION 2

TO SET THE SCENE

Encourage people to see the various ways God still reveals himself to us – through his word, through a sermon, the words of a song, someone else's comments to us, in a sunset, in an answer to prayer etc. Some of these things could be labelled prophecy. Use this opening discussion to put people at ease with the term. Explain that prophecy is not just foretelling the future but it is any word that God brings to mind which encourages and builds up another believer.

1. Daniel emphasised that although other kingdoms and empires would come after Nebuchadnezzar's, ultimately God's kingdom would be triumphant. The inevitability and the guaranteed victory of God's kingdom is key. We know that no human power or system can stand in the way of God's rule (2:44).

2. The Israelites would be encouraged that although they were in exile now they would not always be in such disgrace. Ultimately, their God would triumph even though he seemed impassive to their pleas. He had allowed Nebuchadnezzar control but he would depose him in due course. Regardless of the political or social scene God was still in control.

3. Chapter 7 parallels chapter 2 using imagery of beasts rather than empires. We learn that Christians will be oppressed but after a time evil will be decisively defeated and believers will rule with Christ. The Messiah will be in charge of this final kingdom. He will be brought before God's throne, given the prize of universal rule and be worshipped forever. The Messiah is described as 'like a son of man' – the term Jesus used about himself to explain his heavenly yet human status.

4. a) In the New Testament prophecy seemed to be spontaneous promptings by the Holy Spirit, messages that God put on people's hearts to share with others. Sometimes prophecy predicted the future as in Acts 21:10–11, but it was also concerned with the disclosure of sins (1 Cor. 14:25). Any word which edified believers could be called prophecy (1 Cor. 14:3). 1 Thessalonians 5:19–21 and 1 Corinthians 14:29–33 suggest a word of caution indicating that prophecy had to be tested and rejected if necessary. It was to be an encouragement to believers and also to lead unbelievers to God (1 Cor. 14:23–25). b) Different groups and individuals will come up with different answers perhaps depending on denominational background and tradition so be sensitive to others' views. Encourage the group to determine how much of the New Testament church's experience of prophecy should be normative for us. Recognise that even if we don't call it prophecy, prophecy does happen in non-charismatic churches. For example, someone might feel burdened to pray for a particular missionary in the prayer meeting, another might say a word of comfort which really hit the target in an individual's life, another might be prompted by God to give out a particular song or read a certain passage of Scripture which is pertinent to the congregation.

5.   As a church community we can be a voice to our culture, speaking out against injustice, immorality etc. The way we relate to one another and love one another should be a signpost to the world of what living under God's rule will be like. Our lifestyle and message should have the same effect as the Old Testament prophets challenging those outside God and calling them to make a decision.

6.   Different group members may have different views here. There is a biblical mandate to obey authorities (Rom. 13:1–7) unless they are advocating something ungodly (Acts 5:29). There is also the biblical precedent to work hard within the political system until it impinges on loyalty towards God – for example Joseph, Daniel, and Nehemiah. However, we should not expect that utopia will arrive simply because Christians are involved in politics – only Christ's return will bring the degree of society transformation we long for.

7.   Knowing the outcome of the dream did not eliminate Daniel's fears (7:15, 28). In a similar way although we know God's ultimate triumph was secured at the cross (Col. 2:15) we still have to live with the effects of evil in the present age. Evil is still a real and present danger – we should not minimise it and where possible we need to address it. But because we know its power is temporary we shouldn't be over-whelmed by it. To some extent we can combat evil by godly living (Col. 3:5–17) and by drawing on spiritual resources (Eph. 6:10–18).

8.   In a small way each Christian's life and work brings the kingdom of God to earth now. As we reflect Christ's values and ethics, his kingdom is established (Mark 1:15). Therefore, what we do now does have long-term value and significance (1 Cor. 3:12–15, 15:58). Knowing that what we do matters to God and influences others who watch our lives will motivate us to be more like Jesus.

9.   Encourage each of the group members to be specific here.

SESSION 3

TO SET THE SCENE

We may not be required to worship a golden statue but like Daniel and his friends we live in a world where there is a core set of beliefs and an accepted code of practice which sits uncomfortably with the Christian faith. We may be vaguely aware of these ideas and concepts but this exercise will actually enable us to articulate them. Discuss where these ideas impact your life at home and at work.

1. It seems the decision was driven by the friends' personal relationship with God - they kept calling him 'our God'. Bowing down would have meant pledging allegiance and obedience to a foreign God (3:28). Perhaps their public act was also to set an example to the other Israelites.

2. Encourage people to draw from their own personal experience and to come up with a number of different options to deal with the various scenarios. In each case, if you choose to give an explanation what exactly would you say? Similarly if you choose to remain silent, what rationale would you use?

3. The furnace was seven times hotter than normal (3:19); the strongest men were commanded to tie the friends up (3:20); the men were thrown into the furnace with all their clothes on which would fuel the fire (3:21); simply delivering the men to the furnace killed the guards (3:22).

4. Perhaps God wanted to remind the friends that although the exile seemed to indicate he had been overpowered, he was very much alive and would defend his honour (3:15). Perhaps God wanted the friends to know that loyalty and obedience to him would be rewarded.

5. Job 2:3 shows that persecution can clarify the grounds of our faith proving that it is genuine rather than merely an attempt to gain God's favour and blessing. Paul's example in 2 Corinthians 12 demonstrates that difficulties helps us retain an honest assessment of ourselves, forcing us to rely on God's grace and enabling us to showcase God's power. Hebrews 12 reveals how persecution can be proof of God's love for us as his discipline helps us become more Christ-like, producing in us righteousness and peace. 1 Peter 1 encourages us to persevere through persecution until our faith is refined and proven to be genuine, bringing God glory and releasing joy.

6. Invite the group to share examples of what God has taught them. Discuss how God's faithfulness in the past helps us cope with new troubles and challenges. Be sensitive that some group members may be going through difficulties or have past issues that they find hard to talk about.

7. Try and come up with practical ways the church in the West can show solidarity with those who are being persecuted. How best can we pray for them; what action either political or social can we take; what can we learn from their example?

8. Share your views on this subject. Are Christians in the West being persecuted? Are there signs that full-blown persecution will come? If there are areas where our faith is being marginalised to what extent should we be more active and vocal?

SESSION 4

Take care to watch your timings for this study to allow time to worship at the beginning and end of the session.

TO SET THE SCENE

Acquiring control and staying in control are crucial issues in our generation. Getting on in our careers, earning money and even how we relate to family members often revolve around issues of control. Use this opening exercise to discuss how the people think about their lives and who controls them.

1. Initially the king made bold statements that seemed to honour God (2:46–49) but his commissioning of the statue indicates he had not really repented or understood the central place God wanted to have in his life. It seems that the king was happy for God to be just one of the pantheon of other gods he worshipped. After the fiery furnace episode Nebuchadnezzar seemed impressed by God's power (3:29) but his heart was not touched – he was still content with his own achievements (4:28–30). It was only when Nebuchadnezzar had first-hand experience of God, being sent to roam about like a wild animal, that he realised that God wanted to deal with him personally. After this incident we see a humble man who recognised God's rightful place in his life and who recognised that any achievements were gifts of God's grace (4:36–37).

2. Encourage people to reflect on what verse 17 means today. Knowing God is in control of our political scene can give us comfort, peace and stability. Terrorism may seem to be winning but God is in control; he sees the bigger picture, allows certain men to ascend for a while but will ultimately triumph.

3. You may exercise authority as a parent, employer/manager, Sunday school teacher, prefect, church/ministry leader. Examine your own leadership – do you exercise it with grace knowing it has been given by God or do you have controlling tendencies? Do you act as if the ministry you're involved in is yours or God's? Do you hold on tightly to the trappings of power? Do you easily forgive and give people a second chance?

4. This is a difficult question. 'Heaven rules' now in the sense that God is sovereign and he is in control of all that happens. He gives freedom to individuals and this includes freedom to sin if they choose. This is not what God would choose for humanity but he is able to incorporate this into his cosmic plan. However, we should pray that as individuals we would do God's will and be obedient to him. This would bring him great pleasure and be a positive contribution to his purposes in the world.

5. At the end of each of the first six chapters of Daniel God's faithfulness to his exiled people is underlined. Despite hardships and persecution each of the chapters ends on a positive note. The exiled people are given examples that God is in control and active on their behalf and despite refusing the king's food Daniel and his friends excel in the Babylonian academy and we learn of Daniel's long tenure at court (chapter 1). Daniel interprets the king's dream and he and his friends are honoured with gifts and positions (chapter 2). The friends are rescued from the fiery furnace and the king acknowledges God (chapter 3). After a period of insanity Nebuchadnezzar expresses his devotion to God (chapter 4). Belshazzar the pagan king is killed and Daniel is promoted (chapter 5). King Darius acknowledges God and Daniel prospers (chapter 6).

6. Invite the group to share how they have learnt about God's sovereignty – perhaps it has been by watching someone else's life, by suffering a bereavement or serious health problem, or seeing God orchestrate events at a crucial point in life.

7. Perhaps your Babylon is your ministry achievements, the success of your church plant or healthy church growth, for example. It could be your accomplishments at work that give you a certain status and lifestyle. It could be your children who have grown up and are doing well for themselves. We can make Babylons out of anything because we are too eager to look for security and approval outside God.

8. Like Nebuchadnezzar (see 4:26–30, 36–37) we need to see our position in society and all our achievements as being granted by God. All that we are, have and do are gifts of God's grace to us. They are nothing to boast of but only more reasons to be grateful to God and depend on him. God can easily humble us or raise us up like the king. Clearly God does not hate human achievement, wealth, power or status. In fact he gave Nebuchadnezzar greater status than he had had before (4:36), but God does want us to see our wealth and status as gifts from him, given for his glory and aggrandisement not our own.

9. We need to keep humble before God – reading his word, asking for his strength, taking time to repent. Perhaps have an accountability partner or a prayer partner who can be honest with you and help pray through key issues in your life. Practise being open-handed with money realising that God has given it to you to use for his purposes. We can learn from Daniel's advice to the king in 4:27 by renouncing our sins, doing what is right and being kind to the oppressed.

SESSION 5

TO SET THE SCENE

Encourage people to appreciate the numerous ways God demonstrates his power every day. See God's power not just in terms of what we would call 'the miraculous' but also in the ordinariness of life. Your list could include, for example, God's power displayed in a sunset, an answered prayer, the healing of a sick person, a child's growth, a person's salvation, the strength you have to be gracious to another person and to love sacrificially.

1. The accounts seem to be deliberately back-to-back in order to contrast the response of the two kings to God. Nebuchadnezzar eventually humbled himself before God and gained a true perception of his power in relation to God's. However, despite seeing the writing on the wall and Daniel's stark interpretation of the message Belshazzar did not repent or respond to God.

2. Why God saves some people and not others is a contentious issue. Clearly God will deal with individuals on his own terms as he chooses. No one has a right to be saved so any salvation is by God's grace. However, the case of Nebuchadnezzar and Belshazzar seems to indicate that God's dealings with them was at least in part a response to their behaviour. Belshazzar showed no inclination toward God despite witnessing his power in the life of his predecessor. On the other hand Nebuchadnezzar always seemed inclined towards God, respectful and honouring.

3. The king had not humbled himself before God even though he knew the truth about him from Nebuchadnezzar. He desecrated the holy vessels deliberately. By using these vessels he was setting himself up against God, mocking God and choosing to praise worthless idols instead.

4. Encourage the group to come up with as many examples as they can. Some suggestions – using God's name as a swear word; lack of respect and honour; Sunday is no longer a day of rest with church attendance the norm; the proliferation of other religions means we are pressurised to be tolerant of the demands of other gods rather than obey God alone.

5. a) Because God doesn't strike us down for disobedience as he did in New Testament times (for example, the scene with Ananias and Sapphira in Acts 5) society assumes he is powerless and so openly defies him. Consequently we challenge the ethical boundary markers God has laid down in the Ten Commandments. We try to eradicate God as a force behind science. By focusing on the acquisition of money, status and recognition we indicate a disbelief and lack of trust in God's power for our own security and also to make a difference in the world. b) Think through the implication of these issues and discuss people's differing views. Should Christians be involved in these practices – what are the arguments for and against?

6. People will have various views here. Discuss the view that seeker-sensitive services have made church so relevant and contemporary that there is no room for the transcendence of God. Discuss whether our reliance on technology has removed the need to rely on God? What about our songs? Have they become so man-focused that we don't consider the attributes of God, including his power?

7. Perhaps we are reluctant to rely fully on the power of God because that would mean we would have to stop relying on ourselves. We would no longer be in control and we wouldn't know what to expect. Perhaps we don't rely on the power of God because we don't know what that means. Does it mean we do nothing? Does it mean we take a sensible course of action and just pray hard, or does it mean we expect God to act and leave room for him to do so? Perhaps we don't rely on God's power alone because we haven't seen many role models of others who have done so.

SESSION 6

TO SET THE SCENE

Invite people to share what they have learnt from an older Christian – it could be their parents, someone in their church, a work colleague, a speaker at a conference, or a youth leader, for example. Use this exercise to discuss what is most winsome about these Christians and what practical measures and spiritual disciplines we need to implement now to model their behaviour.

1. Brainstorm as many words to describe Daniel as you can and then let the group choose the top three. Possible words could be: wise, a man of integrity, winsome, trustworthy, courageous.

2. Perhaps they disliked Daniel precisely because there was no malice or lack of integrity in him. He was a foreigner who worshipped another God and yet had succeeded well in Babylon, become a confidant of the king and amassed tremendous power and prestige. His contemporaries would have been jealous of the fact the king planned to put him in charge of the whole kingdom (6:3). The text doesn't make it explicit but it is possible that they disliked him because they were challenged by his faith and offended at his unwillingness to worship the multiple Babylonian gods.

3. Under both Nebuchadnezzar and Darius, Daniel worked hard and distinguished himself. The kings trusted him with their kingdoms despite the fact he was an Israelite. In 6:4 he is described as trustworthy and neither corrupt nor negligent. At the same time as excelling in service he excelled in devotion to God and would not compromise his principles. Daniel reminds us to be loyal workers, being helpful where we live and work but making sure the orientation of our life is not Babylon but Zion.

4. Let the group discuss what it means to be trustworthy. Does it mean telling the whole truth all the time even if it means hurting people's feelings? How can the church preserve its integrity and the integrity of the gospel as we try and witness to people? Does being trustworthy with the gospel mean for example that we tell people about hell and judgement the first time we speak to them or is it legitimate to appeal to felt needs?

5. Daniel's habit of praying three times a day 'just as he had done before' (6:10) prepared him when he had to make a choice between obedience to God and to the authorities.

6. Invite people to share their experiences. Does it get easier or harder to share/ defend your faith the higher up the corporate ladder you go, as you get more integrated into church life and lose touch with non-Christian friends, when you first tell your non-Christian family about your faith or when they think they know what you believe?

7. Perhaps God allowed Daniel to face another trial for the same reasons he allows trials in our lives – so that we keep depending on him; so that the secular world can see God's power and strength; so that we and our contemporaries see the value of faith; to keep us longing and focused on heaven; to display his glory through our weakness.

8. There are various distractions and temptations as we get older. For example, becoming a slave to work rather than to God; getting used to a certain standard of living and enjoying all the perks of a disposable income; being more and more involved in ministry and losing sight of the reason why you're doing it, losing your focus on Christ; getting so busy with life that we don't listen to God any more. Daniel prepared himself to be loyal to God by praying. We can also make sure we are reading the Bible and having fellowship with believers, particularly those who will hold us accountable. With these habits in place we should be aware of the occasions where we are in danger of assimilating into our secular culture and losing our Christian distinctives.

9. God had taught Daniel many things. No doubt Daniel would say that God had proved himself faithful; he had demonstrated his sovereign control and shown he was zealous for his own glory. God had taught Daniel that being faithful was not easy but it was worth it. Now invite people to share what God has taught them about himself in the last month or week.

FURTHER INFORMATION

If you would like further information and resources the following organisations will be able to help you:

The Evangelical Alliance
186 Kennington Park Road
London SE11 4BT
Tel 020 7207 2100
Email – info@eauk.org

Care for the Family
PO Box 488
Cardiff
CF15 7YY
Tel 02920 810800
Email – mail@cff.org.uk

Faithworks
The Oasis Centre
115 Southwark Bridge Road
London SE1 0AX
Tel 0207 450 9050
www.faithworkscampaign.org

Open Doors
PO Box 6
Witney
Oxon
OX29 6WG
Tel 01993 885400
Email – helpdesk@opendoorsuk.org

Rebuild
16 Kingston Road
London
SW19 1JZ
Tel 020 82395581
Email – info@rebuild.org.uk

Tearfund
100 Church Road
Teddington
TW11 8QE
Tel 020 8977 9144
www.tearfund.org

London Institute for Contemporary Christianity
31A Sandy Lodge Way
Northwood
Middlesex
HA6 2AS
Tel 0207 3999555
www.licc.org.uk